sugar run road

sugar run road

Ed Ochester

Autumn House Press

pittsburgh

Autumn House Press Staff

Michael Simms: Founder and Editor-in-Chief
Eva Simms: Co-Founder and President
Giuliana Certo: Managing Editor
Christine Stroud: Associate Editor
Chris Duerr: Assistant Editor
Sharon Dilworth, John Fried: Fiction Editors
J.J. Bosley, CPA: Treasurer
Anne Burnham: Fundraising Consultant
Michael Wurster: Community Outreach Consultant
Jan Beatty: Media Consultant
Heather Cazad: Contest Consultant
Michael Milberger: Tech Crew Chief

Autumn House Press receives state arts funding support through a grant from the Pennsylvania Council on the Arts, a state agency funded by the Commonwealth of Pennsylvania, and the National Endowment for the Arts, a federal agency.

ISBN: 978-1-938769-01-6
Library of Congress Control Number: 2014946840

contents

★ goldberg variations

steel city

"change is the great subject of poetry"

and speed I would add   I envy
the poets of New York so many
weird people to see and shops to name
restaurants in which to meet other poets
and complain about overpriced borscht
and I am a New Yorker by birth
living in exile not like Catullus
who was bitter about it but in a city
that boasts The Original Hot Dog Shop
(the secret of its great fries: molten lard)
not too far from a real carousel with real
little kids screaming for joy not too far
from where Maz hit the home run that
beat the hated Yankees in 1960 and that
not too far from the Conservatory with
its statue of Bobby Burns standing next
to a plow whose handle when viewed
from a certain angle looks remarkably
like a giant crooked penis extending
from Bobby Burns' knickers a fact that
has always allowed me to make jokes
about the physiology of Scotsmen who
may be the only ethnic group not subject
to PC constraints perhaps because of
antipathy to Andrew Carnegie the evil Scot
who screwed the workers and then gave them

3

a library as well as layers of black grime
for all their buildings as well as their lungs
a coating still black as priests on
the older structures as now teenagers
make out on park benches after eating
lard infused fries and the little kids
on the carousel yell "MORE!   MORE!"
to their sagging parents as endless
automobiles circle looking to park and
a flotilla of balloons red, white, yellow and green
this afternoon floats toward the empyrean
powder blue above the clouds scudding
before the tireless wind

even as i write this

thousands of my fellow Pittsburghers
are whooping and singing and drinking,
falling into gutters because
the Penguins won the Stanley Cup.

★

Salk discovered polio vaccine in Pittsburgh.
Our people, driven and underpaid
by the evil Carnegie and Frick,
made the steel that transformed the Republic.
Warhol left the city
to become the maggot in the brain
of the haute bourgeoisie. And tonight I spoke
to a friend who said with great excitement
"we're the only city ever to win a Stanley cup
in the same year as a Super Bowl!"

Smile, friend,
but if you smile in contempt
you don't understand
the deep grammar and inner mystery
of your own, your native land, which is
at least as strange as ancient Rome, which
held mock naval battles in the Colosseum,
read the guts of animals to foretell the future,
and whose citizens marched in solemn procession
to placate the whimsical triform goddess
who governs heaven and hell and earth.

The Boiling Springs Presbyterian Church—
a name worthy of Dante—
advises on its signboard
"Pray Hard, Life Is Short"
though it might be wiser to say
"Live Hard, Life Is Short"
though by "live hard" I don't mean
more fucking, money, or booze
though those are estimable things
but more living like a T'ang poet
walking the lonely mountains,
      in winter
         watching snow swirl on rock
      in summer
         memorizing flowers
and if you live hard enough
please observe how the colorful
butterflies as they flutter
delicately sip sustenance
from puddles of mud
from small or great
mounds of manure.
O Boiling Springs Presbyterians,
your God, if He exists,
is a sly One shy
ironic God.

the telephones

Sometimes on the back roads
you see daffodils
at the edge of the woods, the houses
so long gone even the cellar holes
are filled in, the flowers
like antique stand-up telephones:
"hello, hello? We lived here once,
never much money but
the posies multiplied,
how we lived?—out back
a one-man coal mine—
so busy making do
we were never lonely,
but what do you know
about loneliness?"

My daughter calls:
Q. just back from pre-school
snuck up behind her and yelled
"PENIS!"   then hopped around the room
yelling "PENIS PENIS PENIS"
and told her: "Brent is very penis-ey"
"The Science Museum is very penis-ey"
"Granma L. is very penis-ey."
Then: "have you ever seen Dad
without his clothes on?" and when
answered in the affirmative, spun
around the room again, screaming happily.

My daughter says
"we have our work cut out for us,"
and as I hear the kid running
down the hall chanting
"PEE-NIS!   PEE-NIS!   pee-nis!"—
like the Pope's nightmare
about Eve escaping Eden—
I tell her "it sounds as though
the Golden Age
is over."

The campus on the hill
fired Snodgrass the year before
Heart's Needle won the Pulitzer
(years later, in Wilkinsburg,
a borough next to Pittsburgh,
I saw a small tottering sign:
"Home of W.D. Snodgrass").
In my freshman year, we watched
from the dorm window
the glamorous jocks and Thetas
on the Psi U terrace.
Slade Hirshfeld boasted she had
the lowest average of any graduating senior.
Arlene Devereaux, a talented painter,
was drunk one night when she went
to see her boyfriend's Cessna
in its hangar by the lake
and, when he started the prop,
lost her right hand.
Don Moyer told me he loved me.
I was a spear carrier
in a production of *Medea*.
In my fraternity (I left during second year)
Ratan Tata, soon to be the world's
richest man, demonstrated his abilities
by assuming the lotus position
then walking across the floor
and up stairs
on his knees.

I too dislike it
the mystified truisms
the dusty puzzle-prunes
the theatrical exaggerations:
"the brutal crescendo of woodworms"—

yet I think of O'Hara's delight
in the endless pleasures
of quotidian life and Duhamel
throwing a dozen balls in the air
and juggling them all
Frank said only a few poems
are as good as the movies
but that was a long time ago
before a lot of bad movies
before background music before
there was almost no silence and
"the private life" is an insult to others.

Poetry is the most private art:
Li-Young remembering his father
combing his mother's hair,
Stern and Gilbert with their mouths open
walking down a street in Paris, Judith
writing the mysteries of Level Green
and her father's radioactive chambers.

Catullus registering his private ecstasies
and fears while the machine of the state
ground on. Kinnell saying "go so deep
into yourself you speak for everyone."

the damnation of new jersey

Uncle Frank despised it, couldn't understand
why some of our family lived there, though
to me my Jersey cousins George and Sybil
were exciting, mysterious and gay.
Frank hated Jersey drivers and ridiculed
their towns: Nutley, Ho-Ho-Kus,
Peapack, Bivalve and Hackensack and,
had he lived, would have targeted
the endless McMansion miles,
the all-we-know-of-hell strip malls.
Ah Mahwah, Cheesequake, Piscataway,
Secaucus, Tuckahoe and Succasunna!

He told me that where the Giants
now play football, giant pipes
disgorged raw sewage, and that
the local farmers planted their tomatoes
in the ooze.   He did admit
those were the best tomatoes he ever ate.

What can I tell you?
Frank was a plain man, a truck driver,
who loved me and was always kind.
He never read poetry—surely not Yeats—
and would have been surprised to hear
that love will pitch its tent
in the very place of excrement.

my first teaching job, boston university night school, "intro to lit"

The day after Salinger died
I remembered that class because
The Catcher in the Rye was my first assignment,
a novel I was young enough to believe
captured all the sadness in the world.

But most of my students were Boston cops
getting credits obligatory for promotion
and they hated the book:
"kid's a spoiled brat,"
"another goddam whiner,"
"could use a good knock upside his head!"

An older Irish cop
kindly told me after class:

"You gotta remember
these guys never had no advantages"
                                    and
"that Hahvard book bag,
it kinda makes you look like a fag."

dr. zoot & the suits play on the lawn for the 5th annual oldies concert at st. andrews nursing home in indiana, pa

After they've finished "Take the A Train"
and "In The Mood" and launch into
"Beyond the Sea" my mother leans
over the arm of her wheelchair and
whispers "have they started yet?"

letter to edward field

I never told you that
when I was a grad student
at Harvard nearly 40 years ago
I sat all afternoon one day
in Lamont Library trying
to write a paper on the Great Chain
of Being for Herschel Baker's course
on the Renaissance, and that
out of sheer boredom
I picked up *The Hudson Review*
and opened it at random
to a review of your
Stand Up, Friend, With Me,
which the critic said
was a disgrace to poetry
and to the Lamont Prize
(which it had won)
and quoted "The Charmed Pool"
and some others, poems
so funny and sad and true
that I collected my notes
on Elizabethan world order
and ran to the Coop
to get your book which
metaphorically and just
possibly literally
saved my life.

I'm writing this on a round glass table
surrounded by gorgeous blue plumbago vine
at 6:30 a.m. in Key West on May 14 and hope
it's a fine spring day in New York so that
when you leave Westbeth to walk around a little,
the lordly Hudson will surprise you
with suggestions of mysteries
and many happy memories.

P.S. I didn't stay at Harvard long
and I never subscribed to *The Hudson Review.*

conan the librarian

"NO SWORDS" they said and
his 2nd Amendment appeal
didn't work, but still
he likes it here.
All he has to do is say "Qviet" once
and the kids in the young adult section
shut up. And he's fallen in love
with Dickens! —blubbered his way
through *Little Dorrit* as his knuckles
worked their way down the page—
and thinks he'll start *Martin Chuzzlewit*
just because that name is so cool.
It's true some patrons avoid him
but the library's Poetry Circle
asked him to join and he's discovered
he *adores* Frank O'Hara, loves to quote:
"dod painting's nod so blue" and
"Lana Durner ve luff you, ged up!"
Who would have thought this muscular hero
would yearn to be a curator at MOMA like Frank?
And he no longer has to sleep in the rain.
No one tries to steal his lunch
or sink an axe in his back.
The sex isn't so great but dozens of teens
ask if they can friend him
on Facebook and he always says,
        embracing his new life,
"Ya, I like my face in a book."

When I had my "heart event"—
a neutral phrase
that makes "attack" sound
as jubilant as the 4th of July—
the cardiologist said "Ed,
sometimes we do it in our 30s,
sometimes our 40s or 50s, but
eventually we all need to say
'I have to stop being an asshole'"
which I thought, that time, was
wonderfully witty and true until:
A. I remembered telling myself
that when I was 20, and B. it
hadn't done a great deal of good;
I've improved my diet I don't
eat two quarts of ice cream at a sitting

but I can't ignore how
we spend the first half
of our lives building preposterous
value systems and the second half
deconstructing them
not that that's necessarily "bad" if
there are some small joys we continue
to hold: as for example
Britt this morning looks out the window
and says "hey, the raccoons
didn't knock over the birdbath
for once."

the death of hemingway

I heard the radio report
as I drove with my girlfriend
to breakfast at a place
in Cambridge Square
that was very fashionable
for omelettes that year.
When we came back
to Paris it was clear
and cold and lovely.
We couldn't believe
he had killed himself.
Not with a shotgun.
What a way of saying
"fuck you" to his friends
the ones who would
have to clean it up.

We ate our omelettes
and drove out to the Cape.
My fantasy that year
was that the sun at Truro
was so strong you could hold
your hand up to it and
see bones through the flesh.

Morley Callaghan, who boxed
with him, quoted Hemingway:

they always praise you for
the worst aspects of your work
it never fails.

Callaghan's fine book
That Summer in Paris
is out-of-print in America
and no one I mention it to
has ever heard of it.

A few years ago a young novelist
I like said "no one really
admires Hemingway anymore"
and it's true that time
has done a job on him
and his macho poses.

We swam and danced a lot
that summer at the Cape.
"We're always lucky"
I said and like a fool
I did not knock on wood.
I dated one of the Walker girls
and at the Art Center's costume ball
we won first prize from Abe Burroughs
who wrote the book for *Guys and Dolls*
and was famous long ago though
this poem isn't about nostalgia.
Wherever or whomever you are
time will change it.

Sometimes there's nothing there
or nothing left.

Nada he said. *Nada.*

karaoke night at the serbian club, south side, pittsburgh
a haiku

two young toothless men
with enormous gusto sing
"Stairway to Heaven"

google it

Of course I love F. Murray Abraham
and Tom Hulce though the real star
of *Amadeus* is Mozart's music particularly
the Divertimento in E flat major, which
reminds me that the tendency of some
academics to denigrate Western culture
in general and America's in particular
is an odd reaction to American exceptionalism,
since for example when we dismiss
"the grandeur of Rome" so lightly
because it was "based on violence"
we're blanking out the fact that
the Romans were never able
(nor did they usually want to)
erase 100000+ people per war
(Iraq) and weren't most cultures
after the hunters/gatherers
based on wide-spread violence?
e.g. check out the Sung dynasties in China
and the Mughals, Aztecs, Hittites,
Babylonians, Persians, Egyptians.
Did we forget the Old Testament?

Why is it we forget everything?

Why is it that somebody will say
this poem is in favor of violence

not to mention infanticide
and euthanizing Aunt Lizzie?

                              Today
as I drive past the Curry Run Church

its signboard reads "ONE DAY
IT WILL ALL MAKE SENSE"
which means "now it doesn't make sense"
—an   honest preacher for once!—

which reminds me to say once again
that Frank O'Hara famously said
only a few poems are better than the movies
though many of his own poems disprove that
and are a lot quicker too,   "quicker"
the great American virtue whether
in bombing or communication which
is why we love tweeting—even Mozart
might have since as Tom Hulce plays him
he's a bit of a twit as well as
a consummate genius which is
sometimes true about artists. And
remember the playwright Carlo Goldoni
said "he who never leaves his country
is full of prejudices" and our own
Emily said "there is no frigate
like a book to take us worlds away"

i.e. every now and then
any culture gets it right.

an evening with gerald stern

age 82

When I was just a kid and got to New York
for the first time I had an epic under my arm—
a long one—and I managed to give it to Auden
after a reading and even got him
to invite me to tea but when I went there
I discovered Wystan and Chester Kallman
in a deep discussion about cheese.
What did I know about cheese?   In Pittsburgh
we had three kinds of cheese: American,
cream and pimento, so I was dumbstruck
and as I was leaving, Auden gave me back
my epic and said he liked the last seven lines.

Which, in fact, weren't bad.

There's a town called Homer City
northeast of Pittsburgh and the state's
put up a sign that says
"Named After a Famous Greek Poet"
so when I taught in a school near there,
IUP—Indiana University of Pennsylvania—
I had some kids from Homer City in my class
and I asked them if they knew the name
of the famous Greek poet and one of them
after a lot of hesitation said "Homer?" and
I said "Right! and do you know what language

he wrote in?" and that stumped them until
one girl—she was sitting next to one of the
Homer City guys, but she was much more
sophisticated and self-assured—
whispered to him "Latin, you jerk!"

When Pitt gave me an honorary degree
the Chancellor had a fancy dinner for me,
and his son was there—a very nice kid who
was just starting Sarah Lawrence—so
I said to him at the dinner table "I'm in New York
most of the time and you have my phone number
so give me a call if you're ever in trouble
or wind up in jail."
Heh, heh, heh.

Gilbert's in a bad way and Linda
takes care of him as much as she can
but he lives alone.   He has plenty of money
but he suffers from a bad disease: DSA,
Don't Spend Anything.

Miriam's a great woman—so smart—
but I never see her,   I can't go
to that part of Ohio anymore,
I'm sort of anathema out there.
Her husband still teaches art at the college.

So apparently Lucy talked to Liam for two hours
before his death.   Do you know if they
talked about suicide?   The shotgun,

I heard, was his father's.   So many
people loved him.

What street is that? Second Avenue?
There used to be streetcars running on it.
I still remember riding them
on the hottest days in August.

Here's a joke the old Jews told
in the Hill when I was a kid:
guy gets hit by a car,
man rushes over to help,
puts his rolled-up jacket
under the guy's head,
asks "are you comfortable?"
guy says "eh! I make a living."

My new book is coming out in German.
I used to think I'd refuse ever to talk
to a German, but these people are so nice
I'm forgetting my vow.

Have you ever been to Czechoslovakia, Eddie?
Have you ever been to Greece?
Have you ever been to Poland?

goldberg variations

Instead of writing the speech
I have to deliver next week
I'm listening to the music
Bach wrote for his student
Johann Goldberg who was employed
by an insomniac Count who
wanted music through his long nights—
don't we all—and I wonder
what the Nazis did with this piece—
they couldn't disappear the *ur-meister*
of German music the way they did
poor Mendelssohn—perhaps
they renamed it "The Goebbels Variations"
the bastards, which illustrates how
a great culture can sour
in the blink of an eye or
auf Deutsch *ein Augenblick*
perhaps even ours one day,
but enough sadness, how lovable
is the endless invention of Bach
who must have loved Goldberg
to expend such energy and grace
on this music, even though he was
given a little casket of golden coins
in payment by the Count—Bach the ever-
practical—and now I've come to the 31st
variation and the aria, the end, and

must try to emulate him who was so
disciplined in his art and who perhaps
after chatting happily with young Goldberg
sighed for a moment, then said
"back to work"

★★ riding westward

born to sing

Van says he was born to sing,
is singing in the rain,
and I remember my friend Levine
saying most people are born to *kvetch*,
but only a few make it big either way.
Example: most people who heard of Poe
(Edgar Allen) hated him, and not
many had heard of him.   When he died
the only poet at his funeral was Whitman,
who was ignored in his turn
(Emerson wrote an early tepid
appreciation, then backed off).
Later, the French convinced us
Poe was a genius.

As I write this it's raining.
Raining for days.
On and on.
If you want to sing,
do so at your peril.
Here's something you may not know
about Whitman:
after three years as an army nurse
tending Civil War wounded
Whitman finally got a clerk's job
in the Interior Department
at $600/year—real money!—but when

Lincoln's new Secretary of Interior—
James Harlan—
found out that Whitman was the author
of a book called *Leaves of Grass*
he immediately sang out: "fire his ass."
Harlan too was born to sing.

riding westward

Going home from Bennington—
sunny for a change not so humid—
lunch in Troy, NY, at the Country View Diner
where the waitress says "happy father's day"
which seems odd how does she know
I'm a father? "happy father's day" and
then I'm on the road again leaving Troy
a piece of mechanical crap
with New York plates riding my tail
asshole but he peels off before I hit 787
Tim and I had our usual friendly/unfriendly
argument in front of the seminar
I argue for the heart and he
for his love of "challenging" poetry which
often means I think "obscure,"
the speaker refusing to tell
what he knows
                              I like complexity
not confusion
plain surface texture
free of mere complicatedness and
remember what Martial wrote
2000 years ago at the grave
of a five-year-old child:

      earth weigh lightly
            on her slight bones
     she whose footsteps
           barely touched the ground

beatles on the juke

Listening to the Beatles sing
"Can't Buy Me Love"
is like listening to Mother Teresa
sing "Love for Sale" or T.S. Eliot
doing "I've Got to Be Me" and
the waiter here who's not as young
as he used to be either is a dead ringer
for the aging Bob Dylan right down
to black string tie, black vest and
40s pencil-line mustache. Strange
what forms vanity takes but
probably because love's in the air
I remember Rick Waswo saying
a very long time ago "I'd like
to make love to a thousand women"
"fat chance Rick" we said then, and now
a little kid runs up & down the aisles
and stumbles so a large woman
his mother evidently waddles up
to comfort him and a very pretty
young woman in low riders also
bends down to wipe his tears
as Bob Dylan smiles appreciatively
at her ass, above the crack of which
is revealed the inevitable tattoo which
seems to be a cartoon chipmunk.
"Hotel California" is not playing

as I leave and back out my car
worried about a red Chevy very close
to my rear but some guy yells
"don't worry, you got plenty of room,
plenty room" and I do, I think
his help may be a good omen
for us all.
            I used to be very
secretive about my love-life which
compared to Rick's ambition
was only *mezzo-mezzo* but I can tell you
that as a young guy my guiding principle
was (approximately):   "don't
hang out with anyone
who thinks chipmunks are cute."

Gunshots at 8:00 a.m.!
oh, just pre-July 4th
rural Pennsylvanians
clinging to their guns
how they hate Obama
for that remark   they cling
to their churches too
but guns come first
well on to breakfast
at the Milford Diner
where the fat Greek owner
loves to chat up customers
while the waiter in old tux
with string tie and
the waitresses who call you
"honey" and two Latino busboys
do all the work   who wants
to work hard?   we want to be
the happy fat owner gabbing   luckily
the Gideon bible has some
blank pages at the back
so I can write this down
before I go

hambone

Stephen Calt tells me
when I'm researching
the lives of blues players
that "hambone" is
barrelhouse/blues slang
for "penis" and is also
used as a verb.
Aaron Copeland is at least
as important to "classical" music
as Hambone Willie Newbern
is to the blues and
I remember one March
some years ago
sitting in a cabin at MacDowell
at the piano where Copeland
had hamboned "Appalachian Spring"
and was very pleased to be
in his spectral presence
as I one-fingered "Yankee Doodle"
on the baby grand and
a New England blizzard
was dropping two feet of snow
while out of loneliness
and creative impotence
I wondered how I was
ever going to get a poem
out of this.

sent an email to Ross Gay:
congratulations on *The Times'* review
of *Bringing the Shovel Down* though
even in a good review of poetry
there's almost always a snotty little quibble
unless the poet's dead or English
(this reviewer hates "shimmering labia")
"yeah" said Ross "I laughed about that too"
maybe it started when the horde
of "theory" phds rose over the horizon
and poisoned all the books they landed on—
luckily then they started to kill each other off
(we can use split infinitives now)—
but around that time American poets
began to write about John Clare
the mad sweet nature poet lost
in an unjust world   one of the theory people
I worked with wrote a novel (unpublished)
so bad cats and dogs might double over
which deepened her hatred of her
irrational colleagues publishing
poetry and fiction—perhaps Yogi Berra
explained it best (note that "Yogi"
like the poet we call "Homer" is growing
by incremental repetition and now
has an enormous oeuvre)   Yogi said

"in theory there's no difference
between theory and practice but
in practice there is"

michael waters

The Pennsylvania Lottery website
is down so I don't know
whether I've won $76 million
half of which I promise
I'll devote to the poor
so while I'm waiting
I read *Selected Poems* which
Mike Waters sent me and
love the ga-ga new love poems
for his wife Mihaela and re-read
the poems from his early books
the first was *Fish Light*
from Ithaca House the press
started by my old teacher
shy Baxter Hathaway—
wonderful, the odd connections
in our lives—so this morning
when all the news is about
the debt ceiling and right-wing lies
that the country's gone bankrupt
and the antics of the latest
teen heartthrob disposable
booby, Justin Bieber,
there's Michael's old
"Poem to an Indian Last Seen
Floating Down the Mississippi"

ancient music

driving out of Pittsburgh
Brandenburg #6 on FM
Bach sent it to the Margrave
with his job application
that was turned down
the music lost for 100 years
so much sweetness hidden
I heard it first at 18
in the Cornell music room
I'd never listened much
to "classical" and now
scribbling this on the porch
that overlooks the meadow
Veryl mowed for hay
(before his early death,
crushed by machine)
I watch the hills rising,
wooded, and beyond them
mountain upon mountain and miles
and years away the ocean
below the surf anemones
and whelks—hidden, waving—
"on the shores of darkness
there is light"

B&B—every room
stuffed with antique dolls
Disney lunchboxes, tintypes—
living room: precarious lamps
vases, teetering end tables—
a minefield for little kids
keep them out of there
breakfast OK except
for biscuits big as babies' heads
covered with sausage gravy
many jokes among the 20-somethings
about "planking" and as always
at these things much talk
about the rectitude and senility
of the passed-on parents
whose religion consisted largely
of smacking and scrubbing
then my cousin William
the Ben Franklin re-enactor
tells about the time he was
in an LA hotel
in colonial costume
wearing a pair of "gag" glasses
with false eyebrows and
a penis for a nose
the hotel manager

followed him around said
he must remove those glasses
that they weren't appropriate
for the decorum of a Marriott

sunflowers

The ornamental sunflowers aren't
turning to face the sun as
they're supposed to but
Britt's just seen—first time
ever—a yellow-throated warbler

Yesterday when Judith and I
were talking about how
to reduce our work loads
I saw a headline in *The Times*
60 more Iraqis killed by bomb blasts
what's that now, 150000 civilians?
more than Hussein would've/could've

Strange contrast   you don't
know where you will be
but you'd better
see where you are

another down day
read *How I Made $2,000,000*
Between Christmas and Easter
(first rule: lie a lot)
Baron Rothschild
gave the best advice:
"Buy When There's
Blood In The Streets"
(but try to do it).
If you have no money
money's the only important thing
(that's how the boss gets you).
If you have some money
there's 3000 years
of poems, music, art
not to mention food,
Starbucks & Cancun.
For the old French, Versailles.
For the old Romans, Capri & Pompeii.
Plus nature, the murmuring pines
and the hemlocks
still plenty of it
around the ex-rain forests
the former mountaintops
the kaput coral reefs
(first rule: everything's cool

if you have endless
exponential growth,
which means another
nature-down day)

★ ★ ★ new year

my father-in-law
grew up on a farm
but after college

(first in his family)
put on his best suit
and straw hat

moved to New York
for fame and fortune
in 1935

finally got a job
as a copywriter
with a small salary

enlisted in 1942,
air force, stateside
marital difficulties

every new year's eve
his wife went to dance
at the Plaza—

wore a long blue
taffeta skirt on the train
down from Tarrytown—

with her old love
the U.S. ambassador
to Upper Volta

(he'd had to marry
someone with money
to move up in the Service)

meanwhile the doctor
told the copywriter
two cases of Bud

every weekend
were not very good
for his diabetes so

he switched
to two quarts
of Heaven Hill

early morning, writers' conference

After all the brilliant talk
what I want right now
is a little more coffee,
the chance to read a few more pages
of the Ammons' *Selected* I started
re-reading last night and have never
been too crazy about
except for "Corson's Inlet"
(his ramble about rambling,
with its inconclusive conclusion)
and the brilliant epigram "Their Sex Life"
("one failure
on top of another")
and the smartass apercus of "Garbage."
Well yes, and I'm finding some others.

And I want off the dance of death
with all its golden oldies:
"Jumping at the Job," "Bullshit Boogie,"
"Grab the Rings," "Sincerity Stomp,"
and most of all: the endless jiving
about "the new" which my friend
Bob Shacochis says always makes him think
about advertising agencies and that
whenever he hears the words "avant-garde"
he wants to throw up.
Stephen Colbert calls the essence of our

obsession for gossip and lies
"truthiness," so maybe we should name
our other great pathological urge
    "newiness."

Right now all I want is a little more coffee,
a little more silence, a few pages
of scrap paper and a pen that works,
a couple more poems to read as
a momentary respite from endless chat
about all this excellence, excellence, excellence.

epistle to the minipolitans

Many years ago
my friend Bob Watt wrote a poem
in which he said "We should
take all the money from the rich
and give it to the poor" and a guy said
"That's Communism! and anyway
if you took all the money from the rich
the poor are so stupid that in a few years
the rich would have it all back again."
And Watt said "That's OK, we'd just
take it away from them again."

He was just putting into practice
Jesus' advice to give all you have
to the poor, though I now think
since I have more money than
I did then that I wouldn't want to do this,
and can quote Engels on his friend Marx
who said a man's first duty was to provide
for himself and his family, though this poem
isn't about Marx it's about Jesus
(who also said "easier for a camel
to pass through the eye of a needle
than a rich man to enter heaven")
and about all those outraged Christians
out there.

The reader says "this is my last poem
but"—smiling—"it's twenty minutes long"
then reads an epigraph from the *Diamond Sutra*
saying life's one long series of illusions—
which, like his poem,
is boring too

hi gertrude

yeah a signifier is not
the signified and sure we're all tired
of corny symbolification but
the trouble is a rose is not a rose
which is to say
there is no "rose"   there is *rosa multiflora*
rosa floribunda   grandiflora   rosa rugosa
and a multitude each unlike others
some almost unrecognizable as roses
so that a rose is a rose is a rose
makes sense only to someone
inexperienced with roses.
and Gertrude had a garden!

humans are the only animals
to see a rose as a beauty object
so far as we know
a Japanese beetle
just dives for the center and eats
it out and various species of birds
(not just "birds") but robins chickadees
jays nuthatches etc. enjoy rosehips which
depending on the variety can vary from
pinpricks to the size of walnuts—that's
a rose for you—and various fungi
it's hard to know what fungi are thinking
just want to get into host roses and

kill them   and for us
every rose has a slightly different texture
and taste—and the scents nearly infinite

But amongst
various rose botanical classifications are
also thousands of varieties in many colors and shapes
for example   *cinco de mayo   hot cocoa   sunsprite*
golden showers   the fairy polyantha   distant drums
fair bianca   margaret chase smith   cuthbert grant
john cabot climber   frau dagmar hartopp   lichfield angel
queen of sweden   the ingenious mr. fairchild
double knockout   and   *strawberry hill*

"a rose is a rose is a rose"
may be witty to neo-Platonists but
Aristotle and commercial botanists
think not

d. h. lawrence update

Truly happy people don't need to know
what so-and-so ate for breakfast
and don't need to tell others
what they ate.

Happy people don't need to say
how happy they are and in fact
when people you don't know
tell you how happy they are
you know that they're lying.

Happy people don't smile
malevolently
at the folly of others.

Happy people don't exaggerate
their accomplishments, don't
say in their bios things like
"poems in over 100 mags" and
"published widely in Bulgaria."

Old house,
of children's laughter
and tears.
Then and now
the spruces bend under the rain.
The red maple we planted last spring
has survived the summer's drought.
The garden is ready for snow.

I've spent much of my life
walking a few acres
between two unnamed hills.
I shouldn't brag, I know.
So many people don't know
where they live.

Crows, crows, crows, crows
then the slow flapaway over the hill
and the dead oak is naked

after calling our son & daughter
to wish them happy & good luck
we get to bed early but get
a phone call from my mother
who died in April   she doesn't
say where she's calling from though
I can hear laughter in the background
and she says Uncle Frank is making
his famous Manhattans which are
she adds gratuitously as always
a lot better than I was ever able to make—
"one of his really puts you to sleep"—
    and I have to reply "Mom do you know
    that you never once so far as I can
    remember have told me 'I love you'"
    and she says rather sadly
    "You've always been somewhat of
    a fool;   don't you remember how,
    that time you passed out at my birthday party,
    one of your cousins told you later
    I cried out   'My son, my only son!'?"

dialectic

In college the first theme
you had to write
was on the American dream

—David Lehman

it'd be great to live
in a free enterprise society
instead of a monopoly capitalism society
didn't Teddy Roosevelt bust up the trusts?
now the rich guys give the senators
copies of laws they want passed.
when I lived in Madison—
a city named after a president
most historians think was an atheist
but Republicans will tell you
was the Father of a Christian Republic—
we rented an apartment for $70/month
from an elderly farmer who had a photo
of Teddy R. tacked to his kitchen wall
I thought then the farmer was a reactionary
now he'd be a flaming radical
today I'm watering marigolds in July
with the temperature in the 90s
and a wren is singing his heart out
talk about free enterprise he's got
three or four nests inside half an acre
something to really crow about though unlike
roosters and various demagogues
wrens of course don't crow

at the farm store

The owner,
a clever woman
who works hard
and is prosperous
blonde and pretty
tells her friend

"O the figs
are all gone
from the vine
outside my bedroom.
You have no idea
how wonderful
it was to wake up
and open the window
and eat one."

at a country diner

Elderly couple walk in,
sit down, guy stands up
to see the menu board better,
wife squints at it from table.
"ONION RINGS" he says
"they got ONION RINGS
with the BLT   on a SPECIAL."
"WHAT?" she says.
"ONION RINGS!"
"I LIKE THEM WITH KETCHUP"
she says, "I THINK I'LL GET THAT."
They're two booths away but
her perfume already is
very thick around me. "THEY CUT
OFF HIS SOCIAL SECURITY
FOR 18 MONTHS"   and then
"A .38 SPECIAL WITH A BEAUTIFUL
WALNUT TIGER-STRIPED STOCK,"
while she nods. Nods again.
The waitress comes over and
says "Know what you want?"
The wife says "I FORGOT!" and then
"OH, I REMEMBER—THE BLT SPECIAL."
The waitress tries to be helpful:
"THAT COMES WITH ONION RINGS."

"Honey," the wife says,
smiling sweetly, "I'm not
deaf you know."

what you should know
about the emperor nero

1. Think of the worst open mic reading you've ever
    attended and then multiply it by a thousand to have a
    vague idea of the impenetrable boredom, the idiocy of a
    poetry reading by Nero, who was devoted to the arts
    and would require your presence at performances that
    stretched for hours, sometimes days, as the pudgy little
    bugger strutted on stage with his lyre.

2. He had no trouble getting published, and won
    numerous poetry prizes.

3. At his readings people fell over and feigned death so
    they could be carried out by their slaves while others,
    like untenured American professors, swooned in false
    ecstasy.

4. Remember this the next time a scrawny kid with a
    guitar and suspicious stains on his jeans stands up and
    says "I'd like to sing you a few poems about Jesus."

5. Despite what you've heard he wasn't very successful
    at rounding up Christians to feed to the lions.   Mainly
    some poor gapers who didn't know enough to come in
    from the rain.

6. Thus Nero is directly responsible for 2000 years of
    guilt and bad sex, not to mention pogroms, hundreds of

thousands of deaths in the Crusades, dozens of popes named Innocent, the massacres in Piedmont, John Milton, the Spanish Inquisition and Pat Robertson.

7.   Also the Emperor Constantine's fib about seeing a cross in the sky and the words *in hoc signo vinces* ("in this sign, conquer") which later became the slogan for Pall Mall cigarettes.

8.   Nero was probably **not** responsible for burning down Rome, which after all would not be in his particular interest.

9.   Nor could he fiddle.

10.   He also failed at numerous attempts to murder his mother, who had poisoned his stepfather Claudius so that Nero could ascend to the throne, but was always nagging him about his deportment, such as pissing off the nobles by holding perfectly disgraceful orgies of a sort distinctly unRoman.

11.   He tried various gambits.   His most inventive: the construction of a collapsible ship which he gave his mother as a birthday present, and which fell apart when she went for a sail.

12.   Imagine his frustration and chagrin when she managed to swim to shore, and he was forced to have her unartistically strangled.

13.   When his stern nemesis Galba approached with an
       army and all was lost, Nero asked his one remaining
       faithful slave to run him through with his own sword,
       after declaring in a grand theatrical manner   "what a
       talent the world now loses."

       Now there, friends, was a poet.

a little avant-garde

I'm reading a writer who has awakened from false consciousness, from being free to purchase the snappiest chips and tasteless beer widely advertised with images of silver locomotives, to understanding that that is the only way he is free. So he has awakened in hell, and he is it.

Often in our culture such revelation leads to a study of Scripture and a refreshed knowledge that the world is only 3000 or 6000 years old, that our first ancestor while living with the dinosaurs was so punished for being tricked by his rib that all his progeny were infected with death by a loving god.

But not our writer! He wakens from false consciousness into a disappeared world where nothing is left but his own clever tongue, and shadows drifting across a landscape like Dresden after the firebombings. Disappeared: love, sex, work, trust, justice, joy, nature. Nothing left but moving tongue desolation, desolation so complete the tongue is without irony.

Imagine him locked in a room with nothing to read but Hemingway, heroic stories of slaughtering large beasts, and honor, and elaborate justifications for leaving a succession of wives, and the purity of work, and his clever praise of Gertrude Stein and his knives in her back. This would mean nothing to our writer,

nor would he think it better than these his current subjects: sharpening pencils until they're worn away, describing the pinkeye of a wife he can't remember marrying, zombie-walking through a mall of gadgeteering teenagers who instinctively avoid him.

Well, he's on to something. He has a famous agent. I see his stories in all the little magazines.

emails from and to afaa weaver

Ed,

I was thinking about you the other day
when I left my acting class
(I'm still working on my play *Fences*,
building my character Troy Maxon).
Anyway I was thinking about you and baseball.
My father loved it as do you.
So as part of my work on Maxon
I signed up for MLB TV this week.
My father would come home from the steel mill
and stretch out across his bed in the evening
his radio turned to a game.
I was watching the Cardinals and Mets
the other day, moving around between my work table
and the kitchen, watching and listening and
remembering how things were.   It's funny, too,
reading about how August Wilson
moved away from Pittsburgh and
the world of his plays began to speak to him.
I feel that way about Baltimore now.

I feel good about *City of Eternal Spring*
and it's coming along.   It's leading me back
to what I know of Baltimore and being in that life
in the factory, using the past and treasuring it
rather than trying to forget it or live in it.

Yesterday the announcer in one game said
pitchers don't try to deceive anymore. Now
it's all about speed. . .I suppose rhythm too.
That says a lot about our world, I guess.

★ ★ ★ ★ ★ ★

Hi Mike,

Amazing coincidence: I'm at Bennington now
and decided yesterday that I want to hear
Pirate games, so I signed up for MLB audio.
It's true what you say about speed—but some
pitchers still know how to deceive.
Our closer, Grilli, is a guy with a good fastball
who also can mix it up.
Your father knew about curves and sliders.
I've said it before that speed is
something I like in poetry—not just
speed for its own sake,   speed to get
to the heart of things and not just fuck around,

Speaking of curveballs: in her new book
Daisy Fried has a speaker with an advice column
called "Ask the Poetess"   who refers to all poets
as "poetesses" and observes that one of the great
recent poetesses is Charles Bukowski.

I'm just reading Don Hall's *The Back Chamber*.
Among other things: lots of baseball in it,
including a really good poem called "Meatloaf."

You'd love it, I think, and so would your father.
Old Baltimore. Old Pittsburgh. Old New York.
Time turns pain to silver, garbage to gold.

bluebird

her nestbox
blown down
by the wind
two blue eggs
broken

now she's
on a dead branch
looking for food
in the grass

what she tells us
about sorrow
about joy

for britt

Dec. 16, Beethoven's birthday

Beethoven is such a great composer but
his personality is questionable which
shows once again that one is
what one does—music, poems, or even
money have claims but also such
unremarked acts as feeding sparrows
in winter which God doesn't do too well—
though we're told He notes the fall
of every one—so that as I park the car
your sparrows in the snow-covered forsythia
greet the weak sun with a matrix of cheeping,
dozens of them, not from gratitude but
perhaps from overflowing joy

★ ★ ★

acknowledgments

For their useful suggestions for this book, many thanks to Mike Simms, Judith Vollmer, and Britt Horner.

Some of these poems (several with changes) have appeared or are forthcoming in the following magazines:

Agni: "For Britt" and "Goldberg Variations"

American Poetry Review: "The Damnation of New Jersey" and "New Year"

Barrow Street: "What You Should Know about the Emperor Nero"

Boulevard: "Steel City"

Chiron Review: "Epistle to the Minipolitans," "Time Capsule," and "Market Report"

City Paper: "That Time"

Consequence: "Sunflowers" and "Dialectic"

Cortland Review (online): "An Evening with Gerald Stern"

Florida Review: "Conan the Librarian" and "Ross Gay"

Gettysburg Review: "Michael Waters"

Great River Review: "Dr. Zoot and the Suits," "Riding Westward," "Messages," "September Rain," "The Telephones," and "A Little Avant-Garde"

Green Mountains Review: "Emails from and to Afaa Weaver"

Miramar: "Hambone," "Born to Sing," and "Google It"

Monarch Review: "First Teaching Job"

Nerve Cowboy: "Early Morning, Writers' Conference;" "Letter to Edward Field;" and "Even As I Write This"

Poet Lore: "Fall"

"New Year" appeared in *The Best American Poetry 2013,* ed. Denise Duhamel

Ed Ochester is the editor of the Pitt Poetry Series and is a member of the core faculty of the Bennington MFA Writing Seminars. He has published seven books of poems, as well as eight limited editions, and has received fellowships from the National Endowment for the Arts and the Pennsylvania Council on the Arts, the George Garrett Award from the Association of Writers & Writing Programs, and the "artist of the year" award from the Pittsburgh Cultural Trust. Recent poems have appeared in *American Poetry Review*, *Barrow Street*, *Agni*, *Boulevard*, *Nerve Cowboy*, *Great River Review*, *Gettysburg Review*, and other magazines. Poems of his were selected for Best American Poems 2007 and 2013.

The Autumn House Poetry Series

Michael Simms, General Editor

Crossing Laurel Run	Maxwell King*
Coda	Marilyn Donnelly
Shelter	Gigi Marks*
The Autumn House Anthology of Contemporary American Poetry, 2nd ed.	Michael Simms, ed.
To Make It Right	Corrinne Clegg Hales • 2010, selected by Claudia Emerson
The Torah Garden	Philip Terman
Lie Down with Me	Julie Suk
The Beds	Martha Rhodes
The Water Books	Judith Vollmer
Sheet Music	Robert Gibb
Natural Causes	Brian Brodeur • 2011, selected by Denise Duhamel
Miraculum	Ruth L. Schwartz
Late Rapturous	Frank X. Gaspar
Bathhouse Betty	Matt Terhune*
Irish Coffee	Jay Carson*
A Raft of Grief	Chelsea Rathburn • 2012, selected by Stephen Dunn
A Poet's Sourcebook: Writings about Poetry, from the Ancient World to the Present	Dawn Potter, ed.
Landscape with Female Figure: New and Selected Poems, 1982–2002	Andrea Hollander
Prayers of an American Wife	Victoria Kelly*
Rooms of the Living	Paul Martin*
Mass of the Forgotten	James Tolan
The Moons of August	Danusha Laméris • 2013, selected by Naomi Shihab Nye

design and production

Text and cover design: Chiquita Babb

Cover painting by Grier Horner from his Jeanne d'Arc series: 80" x 45",
acrylic on canvas. www.galleryyoramgil.com

Author photograph: Betsy Ochester

This book is typeset in Monotype Bulmer, a font designed in 1792 by
William Martin. Martin, a British typefounder and punchcutter trained by
John Baskerville, created the font for William Bulmer for use in *Boydell's
National Edition,* an illustrated scholarly edition of William Shakespeare's
works offered for sale as a feature of The Boydell Shakspeare Gallery.
While the font was originally intended as an English answer to the
modern-style letterforms of Italy's Bodoni and France's Didot type
foundries, it retains an oldstyle beauty and elegance and shows influences
of Baskerville's work.

Bulmer was named in 1928 by William Morris Benton when he was
creating revival fonts for the American Type Foundry. The complete
Bulmer font family was completed in the early 1930s for Nonesuch Press
and released to the public in 1939.

This book was printed by McNaughton & Gunn on 55# Glatfelter Natural.